PARIS

PARIS

Madelaine Mautord

CHARTWELL
BOOKS, INC.

This edition published in 2008 by

CHARTWELL BOOKS, INC.
A Division of
BOOK SALES, INC.
114 Northfield Avenue
Edison, New Jersey 08837

ISBN-13: 978-0-7858-2470-1
ISBN-10: 0-7858-2470-7

© 2008 Compendium Publishing, 43 Frith Street, London, Soho, W1V 4SA, United Kingdom

Cataloging-in-Publication data is available from the Library of Congress

Printed and bound in Hong Kong

Design: Mousemat design and Peran Publishing Services

PAGE 2: The Seine at twilight. Today's Paris is a beautifully preserved, sophisticated city where intimate squares and alleys can be found away from grand nineteenth century boulevards and Gothic architecture almost 1,000 years old rubs shoulders with superb modern buildings by some of the twentieth century's best architects.

PAGE 4: The neon lights of the Moulin Rouge, still one of Paris's most popular attractions after over a century in business.

Contents

Introduction   6

Ancient and Medieval Paris: 200 BC–1499 AD   26

Renaissance and the Sun King: 1500–1715   64

Enlightenment and Revolution: 1716–99   120

Two Emperors and the Belle Époque:
   1800–1913   136

Modern Paris: 1914–Today   212

Index and Credits   256

Introduction

Introduction

PREVIOUS PAGE: A view over Pont Neuf to the Conciergerie. One of Paris's oldest buildings, the Conciergerie was built in the early fourteenth century as part of the palace of Philipe IV. In 1358, the royal family moved to the Louvre.

Located in the center of northern France on a curve in the River Seine, Paris is one of the world's great cities, and one of its most beautiful. With its wide boulevards and avenues lined with chestnut trees and grand Belle Époque buildings, world-famous monuments—such as the Eiffel Tower and Arc de Triomphe—historic palaces, museums, and cathedrals, as well as peaceful parks and gardens, it is also one of Europe's oldest cities and has a culture that is charming, sophisticated, and distinctly Parisian. The city itself covers a relatively small area of just under thirty-four square miles, within which are several hills (the highest of which is Montmartre at 426.5 feet) and two islands: Île Saint-Louis and the Île de la Cité. However, if the entire urban area of the city is taken into account that figure is generally put at 5,605.5 square miles. This enormous agglomeration is populated by roughly twelve million people.

Even more than two millennia ago Paris was a successful and populous town. As early as the year 100BC there were about 25,000 members of the Celtic Parisii tribe living on the Île de la Cité. These traders and fisherfolk enjoyed the strategic position of their settlement and grew prosperous, as evidenced by abundance of Parisii gold coins that date from this time and which can now be seen in the Musée des Antiquités. The town's excellent position and its wealth did not escape the attention of Rome, however, and Julius Caesar's Gallic War saw the city come under Roman rule, now named Lutétia.

Under the Romans the city flourished; it began to spread to the Left Bank of the Seine while the buildings and establishments so beloved by Romans were erected—baths, temples, theaters, a forum, and palaces for the nobility. Like other Roman cities it was arranged on a strict grid pattern, centered on the site that is now the Montagne Sainte-Geneviève. The North-South axis, or *cardo maximus*, would have been along today's Rue Saint-Jacques, while the East-West axis (known as the *decumani*) would have been close to the Boulevard Saint-Germain and Rue des Écoles. Where Notre Dame de Paris now stands was a grand temple dedicated to Jupiter.

RIGHT: This gold coin, now in the Musée des Antiquités, dates to around the first century BC, a time during which the Parisii tribe that inhabited the Île de la Cité were successful traders along the Seine. The island's strategic position did not escape the attention of the Romans.

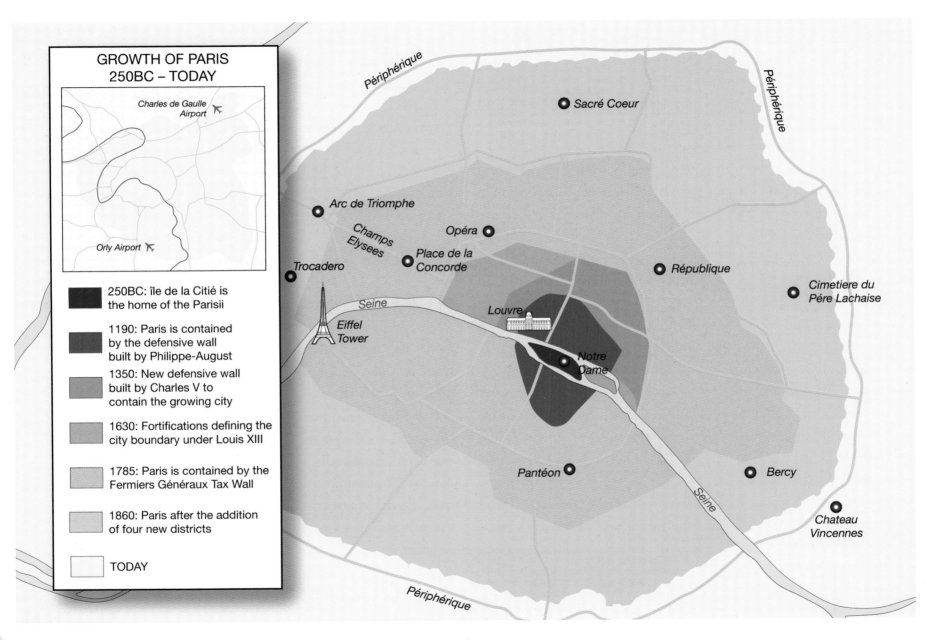

GROWTH OF PARIS
250BC – TODAY

Charles de Gaulle Airport

Orly Airport

250BC: île de la Citié is the home of the Parisii

1190: Paris is contained by the defensive wall built by Philippe-August

1350: New defensive wall built by Charles V to contain the growing city

1630: Fortifications defining the city boundary under Louis XIII

1785: Paris is contained by the Fermiers Généraux Tax Wall

1860: Paris after the addition of four new districts

TODAY

Périphérique

Sacré Coeur

Arc de Triomphe

Champs Elysees

Opéra

Place de la Concorde

République

Cimetiere du Pére Lachaise

Trocadero

Seine

Louvre

Eiffel Tower

Notre Dame

Panthéon

Bercy

Chateau Vincennes

Périphérique

Scattered remains of Lutétia can still be found across Paris, but the following centuries saw the weakening of Roman power, until by the beginning of the fifth century AD the once mighty empire was a spent force and the city, now called Paris for its first inhabitants, was at the mercy of barbarians from the east.

Legend has it that the city was miraculously spared invasion by Attila the Hun in 451 with the intercession of Paris's patron saint, Geneviève, who urged Parisians to pray for deliverance rather than flee. When the barbarian horde changed direction, she was proclaimed the city's saviour.

Nevertheless, Paris inevitably fell to the Franks in 464 and it became the capital of King Clovis I in 508. Converted to Christianity by Geneviève, the king founded the abbey of St-Pierre et St-Paul (which was later renamed St-Geneviève) and the line of Merovingian kings. The latter died out in 751, after which the Carolingians came into ascendance and the capital was moved to Aix-La-Chapelle by Charlemagne. Over the next century the Counts of Paris gradually reasserted the city's political power, though by 845 the city was increasingly under attack from the Vikings. In fact, one of Paris's counts—Odo—would be elevated to the throne for his defence of the city during a ten-month Viking siege in 885–86. While the Île de la Cité survived the Viking raids intact, the buildings on the Left Bank were all but razed, but instead of rebuilding there, Paris gradually began to spread to the north. When Count of Paris, Hugues Capet, was elected King of France in 987, the city again became the capital.

As France settled into being an individual nation, the capital city grew accordingly, with the Conciergerie as the royal residence at its heart. Under Abbot Suger, the Basilique St-Denis was slowly raised over the tomb of St-Denis during the eleventh and twelfth centuries and work began on the competitive Bishop Maurice de Sully's cathedral of Notre Dame de Paris in 1163. The whole of Paris was enclosed by a wall built in 1190 during the rule of King Philippe Auguste with the Louvre in its original role as part of the city's defences, being a fortress on the wall's western perimeter. Sections of the wall can still be found around the city, notably along rue des Jardins-St-Paul. Sainte-Chapelle, built as a resting place for Christ's Crown of Thorns, was begun in the 1240s. Paris also acquired more learning establishments, clustered around the Montagne-Ste-Geneviève. The University of Paris was chartered in 1215 and would eventually be renamed the Sorbonne after the most famous of its schools, which was itself founded by Robert de Sorbon in 1253. Indeed, the division of the city into areas of commerce, government, and learning that persists to this day can be traced back to the thirteenth century. The Île de la Cité was home to religious and government buildings, the Left Bank given over to scholastic pursuits, while the Right Bank was a mercantile hub, centered on Les Halles marketplace whose first covered markets also date back to the reign of Philippe Auguste.

Capetian rule ended in 1328 with the death of Charles IV. The subsequent tumultuous reign of the Volois kings began with Edward III of England, whose mother was the daughter of Philippe IV, proclaiming himself king. The French refused to recognize his claim

RIGHT: This map of Paris and its environs is the work of a seventeenth century scholar and shows the city at about the time of "Julian the Apostate," the nephew of Emperor Constantine who was declared Roman Emperor in Paris by his victorious army. The last Roman ruler, he died during battle in 363. With Rome itself crumbling, Paris was now easy pickings for the barbarian forces that swept across Europe from the east.

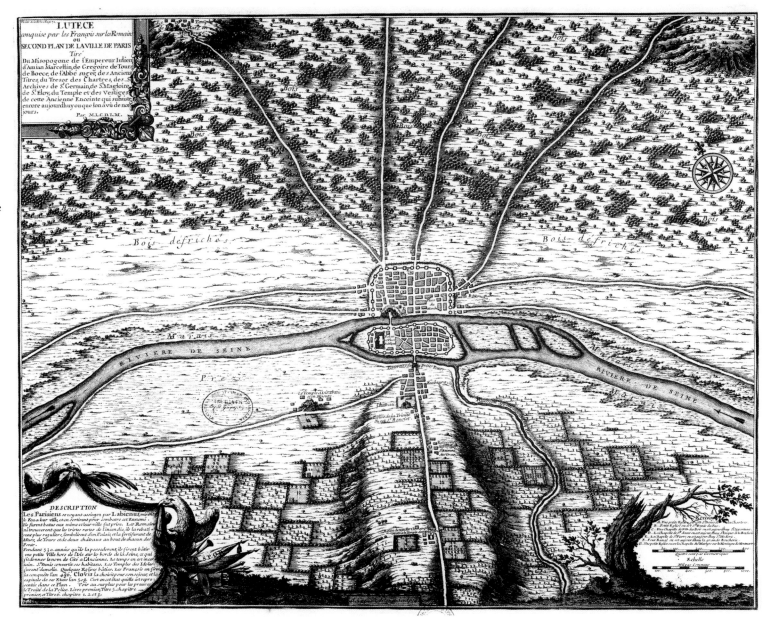

to the crown and instead the late king's cousin Philippe de Valois was pronounced the French ruler. The bitter result of this political bickering was the Hundred Years' War, during which Edward conquered much of France. The mid-fourteenth century also saw the arrival of the Black Death and Paris was alternately devastated by battle, outbreaks of the plague, and political violence. Tellingly, the heavily fortified Bastille was built in these troubled times.

After Charles VII finally took Paris from the English in 1437, he made the city France's capital once more. Although the city would not be the home of the royal court for some decades, the Valois kings set about making Paris a fitting capital, building magnificent churches, such as the Eglise St-Séverin, and Tour St-Jacques, in the richly ornamented Flamboyant Gothic style that is so redolent of medieval Paris. As the city flourished once more its elite built their own stylish homes, such as the Hôtel de Cluny and Hôtel de Sens.

LEFT: One of the most important illuminated manuscripts of the fifteenth century, *Les Très Riches Heures du duc de Berry*, was produced in about 1410 and is a 416 page "book of hours" commissioned by the duke and with many illustrations showing his castles. This picture is from the month of June and shows peasants harvesting Parisian meadows. In the background is Île de la Cité and the count's castle, Hotel de Nestle.

RIGHT: Dating to 1576, this map of Paris shows the city spread out over the Left and Right banks of the Seine. The city's defenses have been enlarged since the reign of Philipe-Auguste, notably during the reign of Charles V in the 1350s.

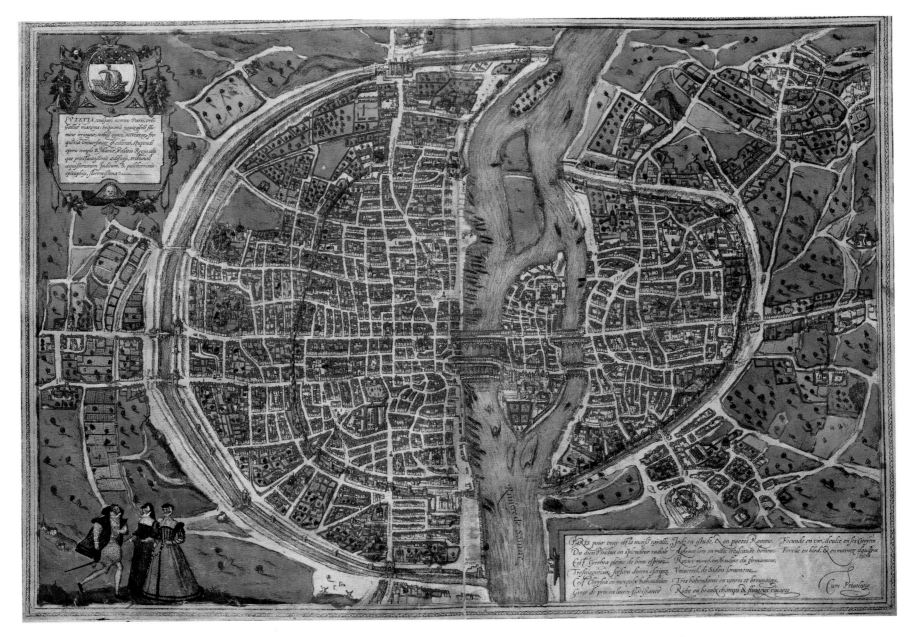

RIGHT: A view across Paris in about 1620. Within the city, growth during this period was haphazard and subject only to the whims of the king and wealthy aristocrats.

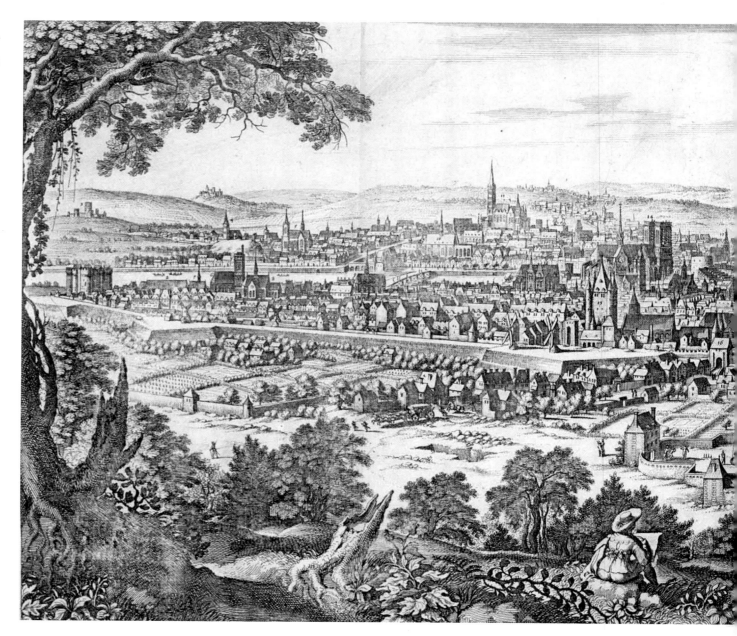

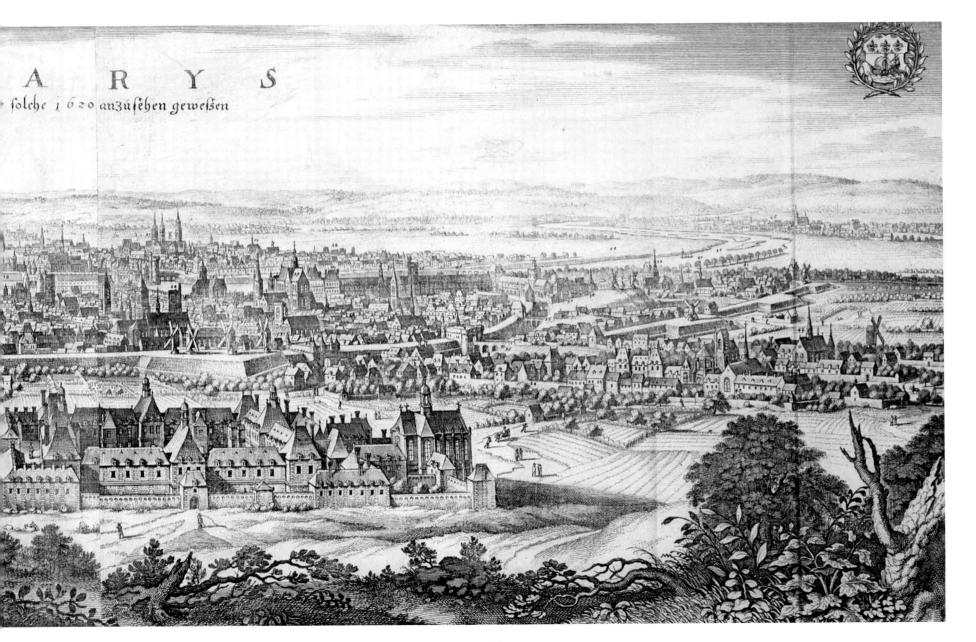

A R Y S

solche i 620 anzusehen geweßen

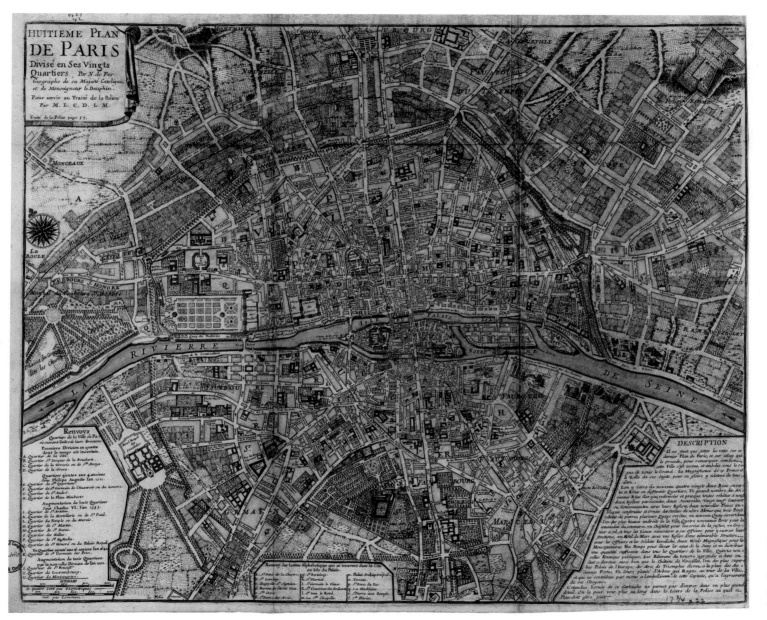

LEFT: This map of Paris dates to the early eighteenth century. The city is now contained within a wall built in the 1630s during the reign of Louis XIII. This extended fortifications on the Right Bank to the west, protecting the Louvre.

FOLLOWING PAGE: The statue of a victorious Louis XIV, the Sun King, shines out in the center of a circular Place des Victoires at night.

With peace, the Parisian arts flourished and the Renaissance finally reached the city. New palaces and boulevards were built around the city, while King François I invited Leonardo de Vinci to Paris and commissioned magnificent châteaux at Blois, Fontainebleau, and Chambord. The Louvre was extended and extensively remodeled. Unfortunately, this flowering of Paris under the Valois line prefigured more bloodletting and political unrest. A staunchly Catholic city while Protestantism spread across Europe, when a rumour circulated in 1572 that the Protestant Huguenots planned to kill the royal family, more than 3,000 suspected Protestants were killed by a Catholic mob. Henri III, the last of the Valois, attempted to negotiate peace, but he was forced out of the city and eventually murdered by a monk. His heir was Huguenot Henri of Navarre, who became Henri IV, the first Bourbon king, in 1589. Catholic Paris refused him entry and instead endured a siege that lasted almost four years, by the end of which Parisians were subsisting on a diet of rats, grass, and household pets. The siege was lifted when the king declared that he would become a Catholic. Henri IV now began a series of civic improvements that has bequeathed the city a number of architectural treasures, including place Dauphine and place des Vosges.

When Henri IV was murdered in 1610 his son, Louis XIII, came to the throne at the age of eight. For most of his reign the power in the land was the infamous Cardinal Richelieu, who brought the country back to Catholicism and left Paris with some extraordinary buildings, among them a rebuilt Sorbonne, the Palais-Royal, and the exquisite church of Val-de-Grâce.

Architecturally, Paris next blossomed during the rule of the Sun King, Louis XIV, though the driving force behind Parisian expansion and improvement was the powerful minister Jean-Baptiste Colbert. The king himself all but ignored the changes that transformed his city— widened boulevards, grand triumphal arches at the city gates, and the new and beautiful place des Victoires and place Vendôme. Instead, Louis ordered a hunting lodge at Versailles to be massively enlarged and in 1682 he moved his court out of the city permanently. It is worth mentioning that at the time of his departure Paris was a thriving city and home to about half a million people.

Despite the degeneracy of later monarchs, Paris emerged in the eighteenth century as the City of Light. The city's salons buzzed with philosophy and intellectual debate and Europe's greatest minds flocked to take part in the Enlightenment. Notwithstanding his preference for Versailles, King Louis XV commissioned various new works, such as the École Militaire and place Louis XV (which later became place de la Concorde). As Louis XVI began his reign in 1774, Parisians now numbered 600,000 while its lamp-lighted, paved streets, beautifully planned gardens, and opulent homes were admired throughout the world. Nevertheless, the city was headed for violent change. Depleted by the French support for the American War of Independence, the country's finances were in a disastrous state and the king, while promising whatever aid he could for ministers, did little but oppose reform measures that would have curtailed the power of the aristocracy. The result was the French Revolution, famously begun by Parisians storming the Bastille on July 14, 1789. When revolutionary fervour reached its

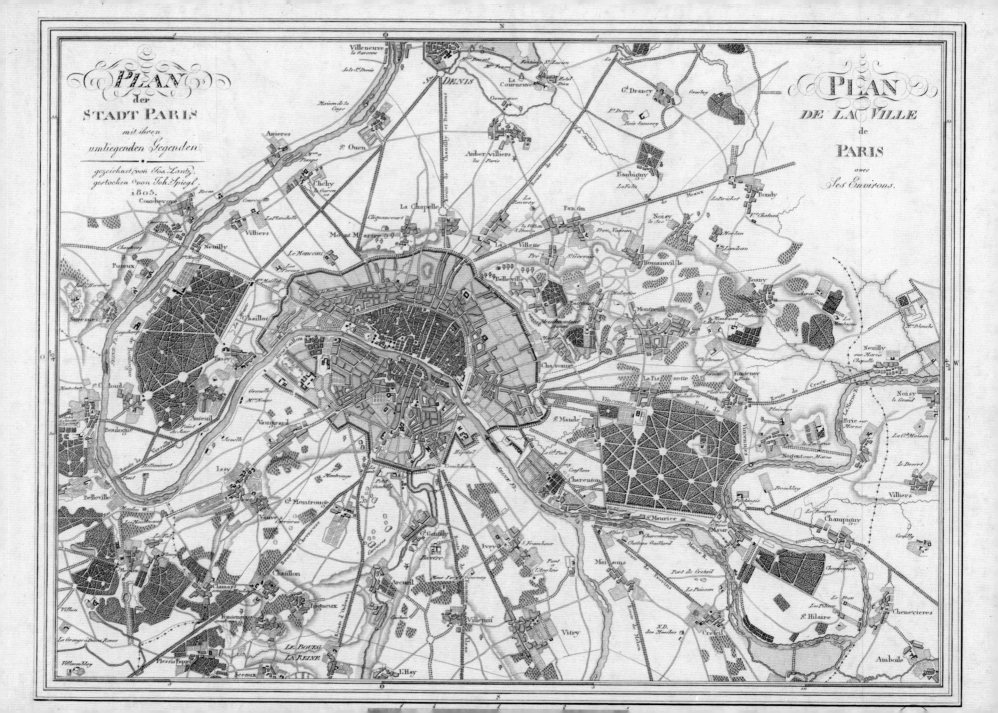

PLAN der STADT PARIS

mit ihren

umliegenden Gegenden

gezeichnet von Jos. Lantz,
gestochen von Joh. Spiegl.
1805.

PLAN DE LA VILLE de PARIS

avec

Ses Environs.

paranoid peak during the "The Terror" of 1792–94, at which time the place de la Concorde (then known as place de la Révolution) and other sites across the city daily witnessed the execution by guillotine of anyone suspected of being an enemy of the state.

Following the Revolution, France found itself embroiled in war against most of Europe. The nation's saviour was a brilliant young general from Corsica, who after a series of bold military campaigns in Italy and Egypt traveled to Paris in 1799 and with typical efficiency, took over the city and the country in a *coup d'etat*. Declaring himself emperor in 1804, Napoléon Bonaparte reinvigorated Parisian society and began to build on a scale to rival Ancient Rome. The Bourse, the Madeleine, Pont des Arts, rue de Rivoli, and Canal St-Martin were among his first wave of civic improvements and monumental buildings. As his armies swept across Europe others would follow, including 1806's Arc de Triomphe, which celebrated his own victories.

Bonaparte's success came to an end with the failure of his Russian invasion in 1812 and finally at Waterloo in 1815. France subsequently vacillated between monarchy and revolution until power was seized in another coup by Bonaparte's nephew, Louis-Napoléon, who became Napoléon III. During his reign, Paris grew at an unprecedented rate, aided by the engines of Industrial

LEFT: Paris at the beginning of the nineteenth century, shortly before the improvements undertaken by the new French emperor. The city had swollen by roughly 300,000 and was now enclosed by the unpopular tax wall, erected in 1785 to ensure payment of tolls and taxes. In comparison to the modern city, however, Paris would still have appeared tiny.

Revolution and the railways that brought tens of thousands of immigrants to the city.

Dubbed Second Empire, it is the architecture of Napoleon III's reign that dominates modern Paris. With Baron Georges Eugene Haussman as his *Préfet de la Seine*, the city was almost completely remodeled. Old medieval Paris was torn down, to be replaced by wide boulevards, and broad vistas. Parks were created or newly landscaped and everywhere were new buildings, topped with distinctive the Mansard rooflines that allowed an additional storey while keeping buildings to restricted heights. The building that most embodies this period is Charles Garnier's Palais Garnier, though railway terminals, prisons, hospitals, churches, schools, and homes across the city all date to this dynamic period of construction as does Paris's sewer and water system, which is still in operation today.

Though the city was rocked by another uprising in 1871, during which a third of the city was devoured by flames, Paris quickly recovered and left the nineteenth century and entered the twentieth in style with two sensational Worlds Fairs. The first of these, in 1889, saw the city's skyline graced by the elegant (and supposedly temporary) Eiffel Tower. The fifty million-plus visitors to the 1900 exhibition were whisked to their destination by the new Paris Métro.

During the first half of the twentieth century, France suffered during two world wars and the Great Depression that swept from America around the world. But while the German army came within fifteen miles of Paris during the first conflict and the city was occupied for most of the second, it miraculously emerged into the modern era virtually unscathed. This was despite Hitler's order that

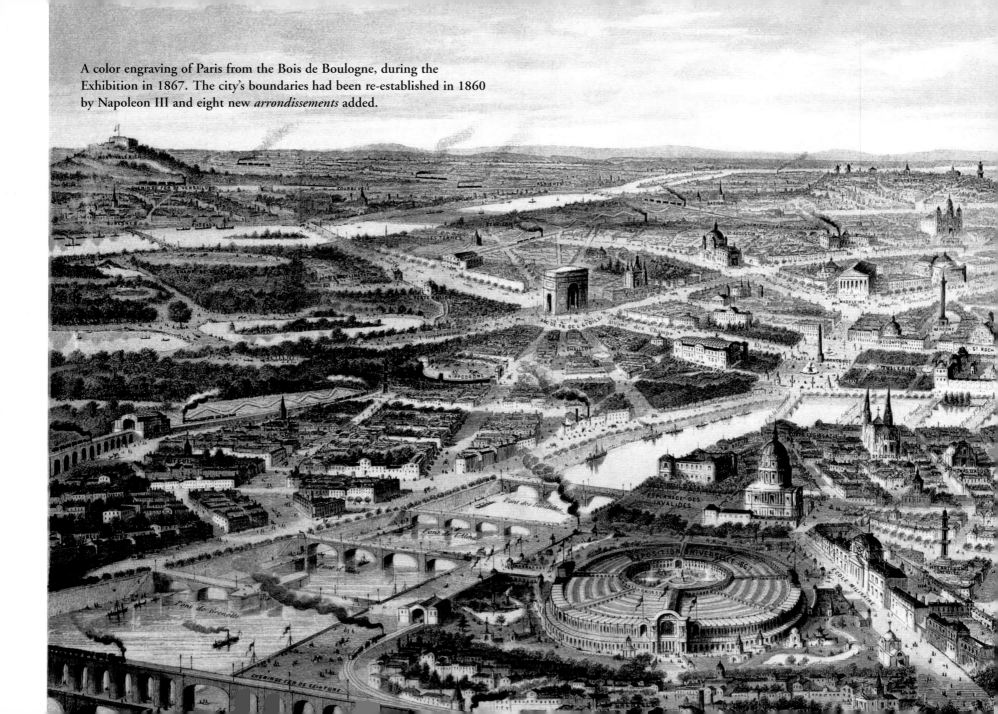

A color engraving of Paris from the Bois de Boulogne, during the
Exhibition in 1867. The city's boundaries had been re-established in 1860
by Napoleon III and eight new *arrondissements* added.

all Parisian monuments were to be destroyed during a German withdrawal: an order that the German commander, Von Choltitz, could not bring himself to carry out.

The remainder of the twentieth century and the beginning of the twenty-first have seen Paris move out into its own suburbs. The city's architectural heritage is now protected by strict planning regulations though new buildings within the old city include such wonders as 1977's Centre Pompidou and the glass pyramid before the Louvre. Nevertheless, most of Paris's most dramatic additions of the late twentieth century can be found outside the old city and include the Grande Arche de la Defénse, Opéra Bastille, and Stade de France.

In the first decade of the new millennium, the City of Light can look back on over two thousand years of history with the pride of a city that remains the cultural capital of its nation. Renowned for its museums and galleries, for its cuisine, culture, and a personality that is all its own, Paris is the world's most visited city. With history balanced against the needs of a working city, it looks likely to remain both important to world affairs and an unspoiled jewel of a city for many years to come.

LEFT: A photograph of Paris taken from a hot air balloon during the Exposition Universelle of 1889, for which the Eiffel Tower was built.

RIGHT: A view across the sprawl of modern Paris. In the twenty-first century Paris is one of the largest, and most populated, metropolitan areas in Europe. Covering an area of 5,605.5 square miles, a 1999 census put the number of Parisians at well over eleven million.

Ancient and Medieval Paris:
200 BC–1499 AD

The Île de la Cité was the first inhabited part of Paris, being home to the Celtic Parisii tribe for centuries before the Romans arrived. In fact, archeological discoveries suggest that the island may have been inhabited as far back as the Bronze Age. Today, the western end of the island is still the center of Parisian government, a role it has played since the first palace was built on the island in Roman times. The eastern end has been a center of religion since the same period. Notre Dame cathedral is built over a Roman temple to Jupiter.

Ancient and Medieval Paris: 200 BC–1499 AD

Although it is likely that the region was populated as far back as the bronze age, the first recorded inhabitants of Paris were the Celtic tribe for whom the city was named—the Parisii. Successfully trading and fishing along the Seine, little remians of their culture beyond a few artifacts, including gold coins that indicate the prosperity of the settlement. Unfortunately for the tribe, such wealth, and the excellent tactical position of Île de la Cité, attracted the attention of Julius Caesar who sent 8,000 soldiers to bring the area under Roman control. Again, there are few remains of the Roman town that flourished here, though from the records and archeological finds we know that Lutétia (which translates as "midwater dwelling") flourished and began to spread out over the left and right banks, within a fortified wall.

When Roman influence crumbled across Europe, the city (now renamed Paris) fell to the Franks. As the seat of Merovingian power the city grew, notably acquiring many religious buildings after Clovis I was converted to Christianity by Paris's patron saint, Geneviève. Nevertheless, when the Merovingian line fell and Charlemagne moved his capital, the city stagnated under the rule of backwater counts for generations. Sacked by Vikings in the 800s AD it was not until Hugues Capet became the first Capetian king in 987 that Paris began to grow significantly again. Now, however, the city made up for lost time.

By the mid-twelth century Parisian had built the grand cathedrals of St Denis and Notre Dame and the Left Bank was a center of European learning. Paris's economic welfare was in the hands of guilds and Les Halles had been established as a marketplace where goods could be stored and sold. The Roman walls had been rebuilt and fortified with bastions such as the Louvre. Attracted to the adventure, sophistication, and commercial possibilities of the big city, medieval folk flocked to Paris and the population swelled. From a low point after the Viking attacks of about 20,000 people, by the mid-fourteenth century Paris boasted a quarter of a million citizens. Under Charles V, a new fortified wall was built in the 1350s to contain the enlarged city.

During the fifteenth century, however, the city's fortunes were reversed. Tens of thousands succumbed to the Black Death and the city was torn apart by political uprisings, while the Hundred Years War with England saw the city occupied until 1453. With war over the latter half of the century saw Paris begin to grow again. Flamboyant Gothic churches were raised while the French elite began to build ostentatious mansions, such as Hôtel de Cluny and Hôtel de Sens. Nevertheless, such growth would be eclipsed by that of the following century.

RIGHT: Partially beneath the fourteenth century house that now contains the Musée de Cluny is a well-preserved Roman public bath, known as the Thermes de Cluny.

LEFT: A nineteenth century etching showing the Celt rebel Vercingetorix before Caesar. Vercingetorix was at the head of a revolt that ended in Gaul, and Paris, becoming a Roman possession. Caesar notes in his *Commentaries* that the inhabitants of the Île de la Cité burned their town to the ground rather than let it be taken. Nevertheless, the Romans rebuilt, and named the settlement Lutétia.

RIGHT: Although parts of the Roman city are still being unearthed, there is little to see of Lutétia today. This photograph shows the remains of the Arènes de Lutèce, a first century amphitheater in the Latin Quarter, which was the center of Roman Paris.

LEFT AND RIGHT: Paris fell to the Franks in 464 and became the capital of Clovis I in 508. Converted to Christianity by Sainte Geneviève, Clovis founded the abbey of St-Pierre at St-Paul on the Left Bank. The abbey where Clovis and his queen Clothilde, as well as Geneviève, were buried was later renamed Ste-Geneviève. Today, little remains of the basilica save the Tour de Clovis, which is incorporated into the Lycee Henri IV. The Église St-Etienne-du-Mont now stands on the site of the abbey.

LEFT: An aerial view of the Hôtel-Dieu de Paris, the oldest hospital in the city. Founded in 651AD by Saint Landry on the Île de la Cité, it survives to this day and has earned a reputation for excellence in many fields.

LEFT: The Bois de Boulogne is an section of woodland in Paris which has an area of 3.266 square miles making it 2.5 times larger than Central Park in New York City. These woods are all that remain of a giant oak forest called Rouvray, which dates back to 717AD.

LEFT: The Abbey of Saint-German-des-Prés was founded by the son of Clovis I toward the end of the sixth century. Built in the fields beyond Paris, the Benedictine abbey grew over the centuries and bestowed its name on the area that grew up around it. This belltower dates to the tenth century and is one of the oldest of its kind in France.

RIGHT: The area northwest of Île de la Cité was once the site of a vast enclosure belonging to the Knights Templar. Still known as the Marais, due to its swampy beginnings, the knights drained the site and over the centuries built a huge tower, a large Gothic church and other buildings surrounded by a wall. When the order was dissolved in 1312 the property was turned over to the Hospitallers and over the centuries as Paris grew the knights' buildings disappeared. The last remnant—the tower itself—was destroyed by order of Napoleon in 1806.

The Basilique St-Denis was built over the original shrine of Saint Denis, whom legend has it was decapitated on Mons Martis (then called Mount Mercury) after vandalizing pagan statues in the city. Miraculously, Denis picked up his head and began walking back to Paris, chanting psalms. A shrine was built over the spot where he finally fell, which became the Abbey of St-Denis under King Dagobert I in the seventh century. Building of the present basilica began in 1136, under Abbot Suger. The Basilique de St-Denis became the resting place of French monarchs and is an outstanding example of Gothic architecture.

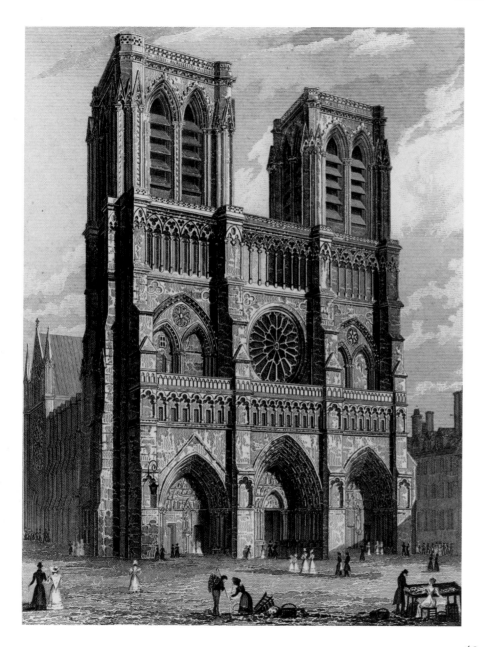

LEFT AND RIGHT: The Île de la Cité is dominated by the towers of Cathedrale Notre Dame de Paris. Construction of the mighty cathedral began in 1163 and continued for 182 years before the edifice was completed. Perhaps the world's most famous example of Gothic architecture, Notre Dame is celebrated in poetry and prose, notably in Victor Hugo's *The Hunchback of Notre Dame.*

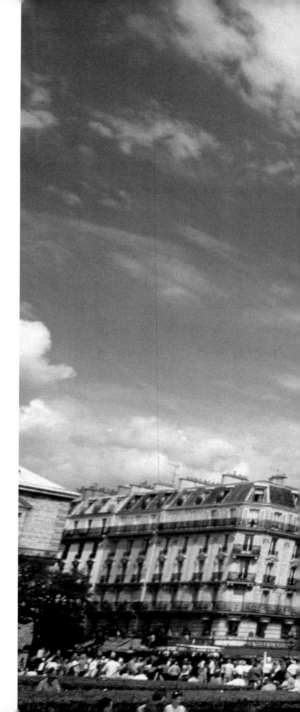

RIGHT: A detailed view of the famous Rose Window in the North Transept of Notre Dame. Unlike many old stained glass windows throughout the rest of France, these windows contain the original glasswork dating back to 1250.

FAR RIGHT: One of the best kept secrets in Paris is the small and tranquil park situated behind the towering presence of Notre Dame. Filled with colorful flowers and places to sit, it has become a popular site for romantic couples.

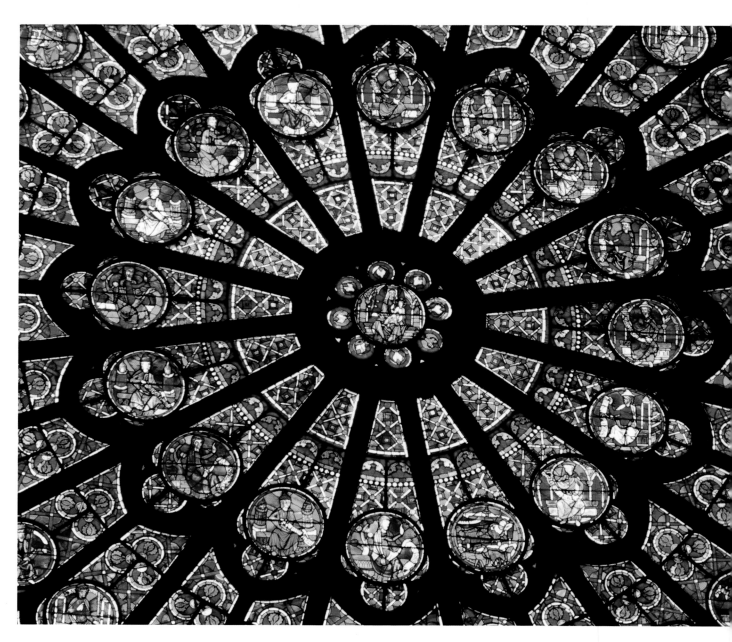

LEFT: Notre Dame's famous gargoyles were actually placed on the cathedral to facilitate drainage, though the grotesque figures are also supposed to ward off evil spirits. Each of them conceals a pipe that carries rainwater from the roof away from the cathedral's masonry.

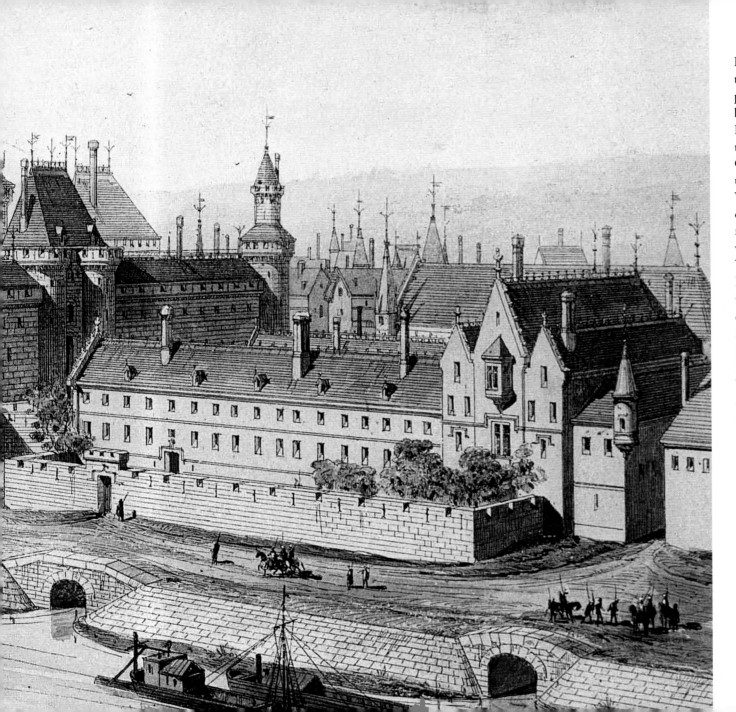

LEFT AND FOLLOWING PAGE: Today the world's greatest art museum, parts of the Palais de Louvre date back to 1190, when it formed part of Paris's fortified defenses. It became the home of the royal family under Charles V in the thirteenth century until Louis XIV moved the court to Versailles. Extended and remodeled extensively over the centuries (most recently at the end of the twentieth with the opening of the Richelieu Wing and the installation of I.M. Pei's iconic glass pyramid) it opened to the public in 1793. The eighteenth century painting is an artist's impression of the Palais de Louvre as it was at the time of Charles V. Reigning from 1338 to 1380, Charles V is regarded as a wise king who sponsored many new royal and religious buildings across the city.

LEFT AND RIGHT: One of Europe's oldest and most highly regarded seats of learning, the Sorbonne can trace its roots back to about 1100 when scholars began to congregate and teach on the Montagne. The University of Paris was chartered by Pope Innocent III in 1215. The College de Sorbonne itself was founded in 1257 by Robert de Sorbon and though it was only one of the many colleges under the umbrella of the university, over the centuries its name became a synonym for Parisian scholarship. The original university buildings are now all gone and the replacements date mostly to the late nineteenth century.

LEFT AND RIGHT: The building of
Sainte Chapelle began in 1240 under
King Louis IX who wanted a suitable
resting place for relics that had been
purchased from the Holy Land,
including the Crown of Thorns and
fragments of the True Cross. Now
surrounded by the palais de Justice
buildings, Saint Chapelle, with its
famous stained glass windows,
remains one of the most beautiful
and dramatic churches in Paris.
These exquisitely hand-colored
photographs date to the late
nineteenth century.

LEFT: Many visitors flock to the towering stained glass windows in the Upper Chapel of Sainte Chapelle but the Lower Chapel also boasts an air of serene beauty and calm.

ABOVE: There has been a bridge linking the Palais Royale to the left bank since 1387. Although the first bridges were wooden and lined with houses, nowadays the "Pont Saint-Michel" is made of stone and decorated with the imperial "N". Its current incarnation was constructed in 1857.

LEFT AND RIGHT: The Conciergerie dates back to the time of Philippe the Fair, who reigned from 1284 to 1314. Originally used as a royal palace, it later became a prison. Though much of the façade was rebuilt in the mid-nineteenth century, parts of the original thirteenth century structure can still be seen, notably the Tour d'Horlage.

LEFT: To the east of Paris center, the Château de Vincennes was built as a hunting lodge for Louis VII in about 1150. Modified and added to by monarchs down the centuries, its central keep is the tallest of its kind in Europe and was built for Philippe VI in the 1330s.

ABOVE: The infamous Bastille, which came to symbolize the tyranny of monarchs, was constructed to protect Paris's eastern wall in 1382. Originally an armory and fortress, its walls were eighty feet high. In later years it achieved notoriety as a fearsome prison, from where prisoners were never released unless they first contracted never to tell of what they had seen within its walls. Despite its reputation though, the reality was that like many jails of the day, wealthy prisoners were allowed to bring in their own furniture, food, and servants and most were allowed to wander the fortress freely. When the

Bastille fell to the revolutionary mob in 1789, only seven prisoners were found inside including a nobleman living in comparative comfort, two lunatics, and four forgers.

RIGHT: With the Anglo-French war over, Paris began to return to prosperity toward the end of the fifteenth century. Numerous large town houses began to appear for aristocrats and clergy. Construction of the Hôtel de Sens, built for the Archbishops of Sens, began in 1475.

Renaissance and the Sun King:
1500–1715

This view of Paris dates to 1607 and shows the city dominated by church towers and spires contained within the walls of Charles V. As the seventeenth century progressed, the city would acquire grander monuments, palaces, mansions for the wealthy, and wide boulevards.

Renaissance and the Sun King: 1500–1715

While Paris was again the capital of France, it was not until 1528 that Francis I returned the court to the city and immediately went to work rebuilding and transforming the Louvre into his royal residence. Under Francis, Paris became the epitome of a Renaissance city, attracting great artists such as Leonardo de Vinci and Benvenuto Cellini while the Hôtel de Ville, and Hôtel des Tournelles, as well as many châteaux, were built and the population began to increase once more. Nevertheless, after his death in 1547 the fortunes of the city were threatened again, this time by religious conflict. Indeed, the Wars of Religion, which lasted from the 1560s until 1594 saw Catholic Paris suffer more than any other city, its population reduced to eating rats and grass during a four year siege that was not lifted until Henri IV agreed to renounce the Protestant faith and become a Catholic. The following century would see unparalleled growth in Paris, culminating in the accession of Louis XIV, the Sun King.

Henri IV set the pace. Paris had been decimated and neglected during the conflict and the king set about restoring it to its former glory, along the way building the first Parisian square, place du Royale (now known as place des Vosges), as well as place Dauphine, and Pont Neuf. When his son ascended the throne after Henri's assassination, he and his chief minister—the famous Cardinal Richelieu—began to construct buildings that would symbolize the absolute power of the monarchy. The Palais Royal, Sorbonne, Val de Grâce, and Palais du Luxembourg all date to the reign of Louis XIII.

Although Louis XIV was crowned at the age of five in 1643 on his father's death, it was not until Richelieu's protégé, Cardinal Mazarin, died in 1661 that he began a rule that would see his capital become more dazzling than ever. Although the king himself was relatively uninterested in the city and determined to move the court to Versailles (which he transformed from a small hunting lodge into Europe's most ostentatious palace), Louis' minister of finance, Jean-Baptiste Colbert, had grand plans for Paris and left it with its first grand boulevards, such as the Champs Elysées, as well as the squares and monuments with which Colbert hoped to rival ancient Rome.

Despite these improvements, away from the grand streets life was increasingly difficult for Parisians. The city's population had increased to over half a million by the beginning of the eighteenth century, and the poor lived in cramped and unsanitary conditions. By the end of the Sun King's reign, France was in debt and the citizens of the capital growing increasingly desperate.

RIGHT: This painting dates to 1756 and celebrates the "Joust of the Boatmen at the Pont Notre Dame." Constructed between 1500 and 1511, the beautiful Renaissance-flavored bridge was lined with houses along its length.

LEFT AND RIGHT: On the outskirts of Paris stands one of the largest royal French chateaux – Chateau Fontainebleau. Many monarchs have added on to the original sixteenth century design of King Francis I.

LEFT: The Tour Saint-Jacques is all that remains of the St-Jacques-La-Boucherie church that once stood on this spot in the place du Châtalet. It was built between 1508 and 1522 and is an excellent example of the Flamboyant Gothic style, which was in vogue from the mid-fourteenth century until about 1520.

RIGHT: Marking the entrance to the Les Halles marketplace, the church of St-Eustache is another of Paris's Gothic masterpieces. It was built between 1532 and 1637 on the site of a previous chapel.

LEFT: The Hôtel de Ville (city hall) was commissioned by King Francis I in 1533 and it remains the center of Parisian administration to this day. The original building was designed by the Italian Dominique de Cortone and Pierre Chamiges, a Frenchman. The building was gutted during the fire of 1871 and though the exterior was largely restored to its former appearance, inside the Hôtel de Ville owes its design to nineteenth century architects Theodore Ballu and Pierre Deperthes.

LEFT: Now a museum housing exhibits that narrate Parisian history from the earliest times, the Musée Carnavalet was originally a magnificent Renaissance town house and dates to 1548. The museum was founded in 1866 on the urging of Baron Haussmann who wanted a place to display architecture from some of the buildings that were destroyed during his rebuilding program.

RIGHT: This contemporary print shows actors at the Hôtel de Bourgogne rue Française during the sixteenth century. Parisian theater started here with the first performance recorded in 1548.

LEFT: Landscaped over the site of an older tile works (*tuileries*) during the latter sixteenth century, the Jardin des Tuilleries was the brainchild of Catherine de Médicis. Originally a private pleasure garden that became a fashionable meeting place for Parisian society, the garden was extended in the mid-seventeenth century and was an integral part of Baron Haussman's nineteenth century redesign of Paris. Today, the garden has recently been reinvigorated in keeping with its original design by landscape designers Louis Benech, Pascal Cribier, and François Roubaud.

LEFT AND RIGHT: These two images show the Fontaine des Innocents in its original position close to the market of Les Halles by the cemetery of St-Innocents and on its new site, south of Les Halles today. Paris's only Renaissance fountain it was designed by Jean Goujon and erected in 1549.

LEFT AND RIGHT: Situated just outside Paris is the magnificent chateau of Chantilly. It encompasses two buildings: the Grand Chateau, which was destroyed during the French Revolution and rebuilt in 1870; and the Petit Chateau which was built in 1560.

ABOVE AND RIGHT: Construction began on Pont Neuf in 1577 and finished in 1608. It is today the oldest of Paris's bridges as well as one of its most romantic spots. Legend has it that the sculpted faces that decorate its arches depict Henri V's courtiers. The bridge was the first in Paris not to be lined with houses. At its center is a statue of Henri IV on horseback, which was replaced in 1818 having been torn down during the Revolution.

RIGHT: Built between 1605 and 1612, place des Vosges was the first of Paris's planned squares and built on the site of the Hôtel des Tournelles. Surrounded by beautifully proportioned red brick and stone houses, it is thought that the square was designed by Baptiste du Cerceau.

Following the Wars of Religion, Paris experienced a fresh spurt of growth in the 1620s. Beyond the city walls on the Left Bank, Palais Luxembourg was built for Marie de Médicis, mother of King Louis XIII. Surrounded by sumptuous gardens the palace was designed in an ornate Italianate style reminiscent of Marie's birthplace, Florence.

LEFT: The plush interior of the Palais du Luxembourg. Now the home of the French Senate, the palace was built in 1625 for Marie de Medici and designed by Salomon de Brosse, the architect who trained the world renowned François Mansart.

RIGHT: The last windmill in Paris, the Moulin de la Galette is situated in Montmartre and was made famous in the paintings of Renoir, Van Gogh and Toulouse-Lautrec. The first record of the windmill's name appeared in 1622.

RIGHT: Palais Royal (originally known as Palais Cardinal) was built between 1624 and 1636 for Cardinal Richelieu, the architect of the French system of absolute monarchy who inadvertently paved the road toward revolution. A grand palace, befitting the man who was the power behind the throne, its gardens were enclosed in the 1780s and continue to offer a peaceful respite from the bustle of the city today.

ABOVE: This illustration of Paris, which dates to the mid-seventeenth century, shows an enlarged city. Recent expansion and building had seen development in the Marais district while the two previously uninhabited islands that form the Île Saint-Louis had been joined.

RIGHT: A photograph of the Pont Marie today. The bridge was named after its chief engineer, Christophe Marie. Seen just downstream from the Pont Marie is the Pont Louis-Philipe, built in 1860, it is the third bridge to occupy this spot. The previous incarnations were burnt down or demolished.

LEFT: The most famous tomb in Les Invalides is that of Napoleon Bonaparte. Napoleon was originally buried on the small island of Saint Helena where he was exiled but, following the massive renovation of Les Invalides in 1861, his remains were moved here and placed directly underneath the famous dome.

RIGHT: Though the king himself was intent on relocating to Versailles, the Paris of Louis XIV's reign became grander than ever before. One of the world's most famous streets, the tree-lined Champs Elysées was laid out under Jean-Baptiste Colbert, superintendant of buildings, in 1667.

LEFT: There has been a "pont au Double" linking the Île de la Cité to the Quai de Montebello since 1634. King Francis was asked to build a small bridge so that patients could be carried to the nearby hospital "Hôtel Dieu." The current cast iron bridge was completed in 1883.

RIGHT: Founded by Louis XIV as a military hospital and home for old soldiers, the first stones of Les Invalides were laid in 1671 and the building was completed in 1676. The distinctive gilded dome was added between 1706 and 1708.

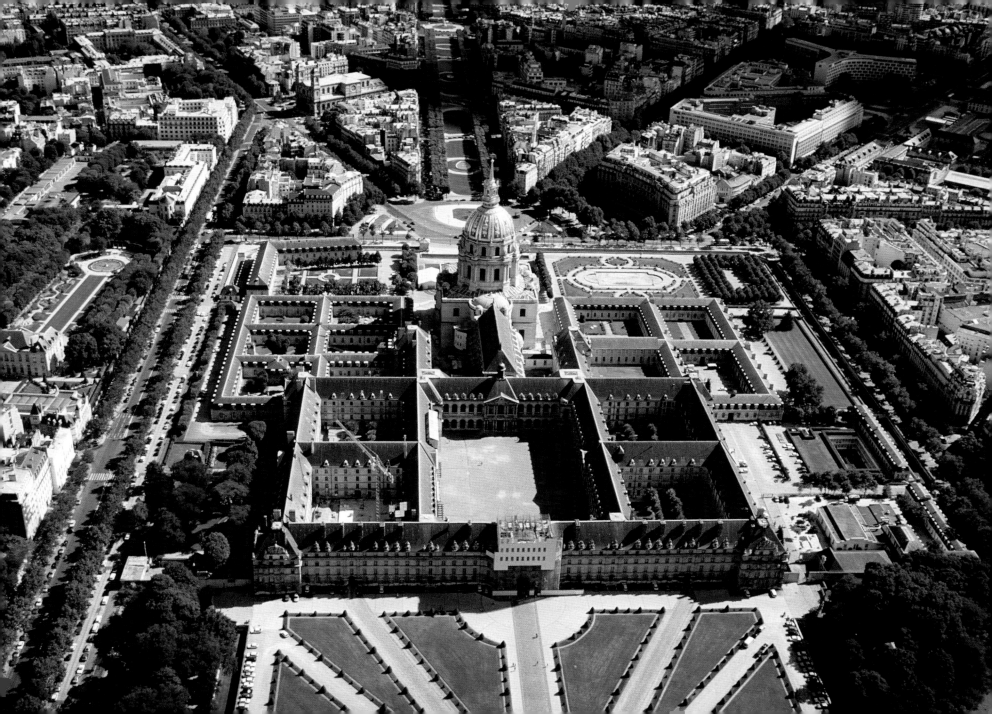

LEFT: The oldest public library in France, the Bibliotheque Mazarine, began life as the personal library of Cardinal Mazarin (1602–1661). He spent his life collecting books and on his death, bequeathed the entire collection to the Collège des Quatre-Nations.

RIGHT: Typical of Colbert's new Paris of wide boulevards, grand vistas, and imposing monuments were the new gates of St-Denis and St-Martin, which were constructed in 1672. This photograph shows the Porte St-Denis.

RIGHT: The roofs of Paris are immediately recognisable from those of any other city thanks to their distinctive Mansard style. Named after the architect François Mansart (1598–1666), this style became popular in Paris when houses were taxed according to how many floors they had but only below the roof. Thus exempting the top floor from any tax.

LEFT AND RIGHT: The cornerstone of Val-de-Grâce was laid by King Louis XIII himself, and the edifice raised on the order of his wife Anne of Austria in gratitude for the birth of a son, after twenty-three childless years. A superb example of Baroque architecture, the church was designed by François Mansart and Jacques Lemercier and built between 1645 and 1667.

ABOVE AND FOLLOWING PAGES: Once a simple hunting lodge outside Paris, during the reign of Louis XIV the palace of Versailles was built into the most opulent royal residence in Europe. A retreat for the absolute monarch away from the disease and clamor of the city, it was surrounded by exquisitely landscaped gardens and lavishly ornamented within and could house 20,000 of the king's staff and courtiers. Louis moved in in 1682 and rarely set foot in Paris again.

LEFT: One of the many extraordinary fountains to be found in the gardens of Versailles. Called the "Bassin d'Apollon"—the Apollo Fountain—it was built in 1668 and depicts the Sun God driving his chariot towards the sky.

ABOVE: The formal gardens surrounding the opulent palace at Versailles were designed by noted landscape artist André Le Nôtre.

LEFT: The fashion for grand squares in Paris was set by the circular place des Victoires, commissioned by Colbert in 1685. Celebrating martial success against Holland, at the hub is a statue of a mounted Louis XIV.

BELOW: Place Vendôme was originally laid out by architect Jules Hardouin-Mansart in 1702 and centered on a statue of the Sun King on horseback. After this statue was destroyed in 1782 it was replaced by the Colonne de la Grande Armée by Napoleon, a column fashioned from 1,250 cannon captured from the Austrians and Russians at Austerlitz. After this too was pulled down in the Communard uprising of 1871, it was replaced with a replica.

LEFT: Still a popular restaurant today, the Café Procope is the oldest eatery in Paris. Opened in 1686 by Francesco Procopio dei Coltelli, the café quickly become a popular hang out for gentlemen of fashion.

RIGHT: The National Assembly buildings in Paris were originally built in 1722 as a private residence but later bought by King Louis XV. The building changed hands many times until 1827, when the French government acquired it and put it to public use.

LEFT: The Classically-inspired proportions of Hôtel Soubise typify the new grand direction that Parisian architecture was taking at the beginning of the eighteenth century. Built for the Prince and Princess de Soubise and designed by the architect Delamair, work began on this luxurious mansion in 1704.

LEFT: The superb Hôtel Biron was built in 1728 and designed by Jacques Gabriel. The house and gardens have been home to the Musée Rodin since 1919 with many of the artists most famous sculptures, such as The Kiss and The Thinker, on public display.

RIGHT: Hotel Crillon, on the northern side of the Place de le Concorde, is one of the oldest and most elite luxury hotels in the world. It was built in 1758 for King Louis XV, who originally planned the building for government offices.

LEFT: The elaborate and opulent fountains of the Place de la Concorde have a nautical theme. This one, the "Fontaine des Fleuves" or Fountain of the Rivers, adorns the northern side of the square.

RIGHT: The obelisk in the Place de la Concorde was a gift from the viceroy of Egypt and once stood outside the temple at Luxor. It is over 3000 years old but did not arrive in Paris until 1833.

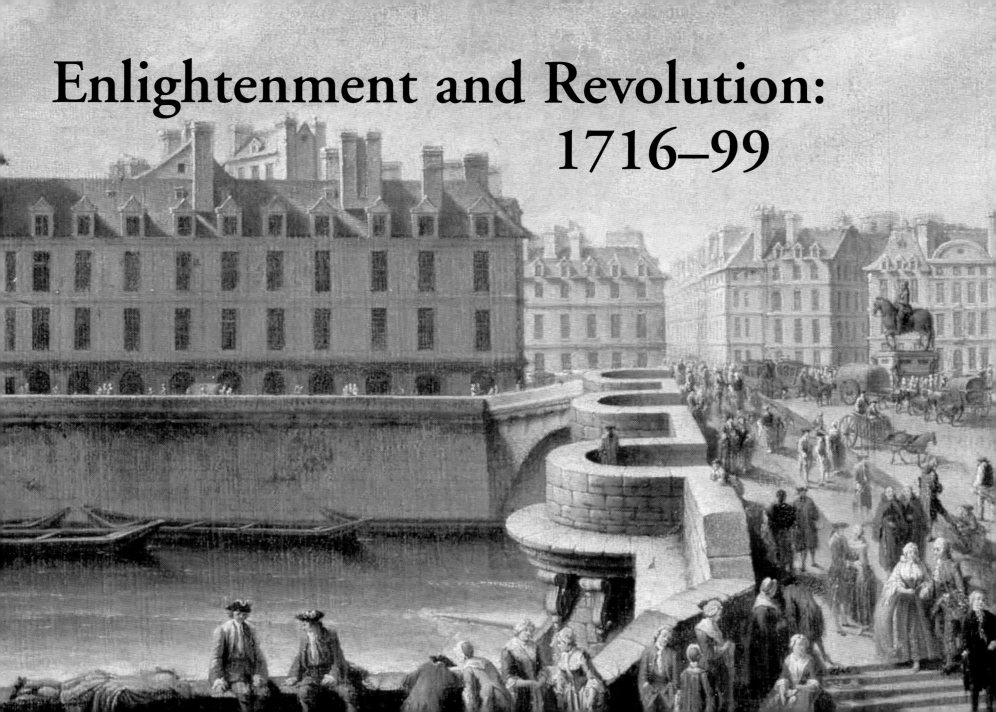

Enlightenment and Revolution: 1716–99

Enlightenment and Revolution: 1716–99

By the early eighteenth century Paris had grown from sixteen to twenty districts (*arrondissments*) with five of these on the Left Bank and fifteen on the commercial Right Bank. As the population increased, the city spread ever further toward the surrounding hills. Aristocratic Paris glittered and, as the center of the Age of Reason, attracted scholars, thinkers, and scientists from all over Europe. Guided by his mistress, the Marquise de Pompadour, Louis VX initiated grand projects such as the École Militaire and place Louis VX (now place de la Concorde) while the bourgoisie built grand houses and mansions suitable for entertaining guests. Paris's streets became the first to be lit by streetlamps (giving rise to the city's nickname, the City of Light) while roads were paved and new gardens landscaped. Parisians delighted in novelty and science, and especially in the balloons of the Montgolfier brothers.

Nevertheless, away from salon society, the city's poor were still housed in overcrowded tenements, and calls to improve their living conditions were largely ignored. In 1785, poor citizens were further antagonized by the building of the Fermiers Généraux Tax Wall, which encircled the city, ensuring that tax on all goods entering Paris were paid. Although these were only contributing factors in the Revolution of 1789, the fact that the city's population were so readily swept up by events is indicative of the popular dissatisfaction at the time.

With the storming of the Bastille on July 14, 1789, Paris's growth stopped overnight. Now monuments and churches were pulled down rather than erected and among the few new constructions on Parisian streets were the infamous guillotines that took an estimated 20,000 lives during "The Terror" of 1792–94.

The final years of the eighteenth century were chaotic. France and Paris struggled to cope under the rule of a self-appointed five-man Directorate and the country found itself at war with its neighbors, whose royal heads of state were appalled by the execution of the French aristocracy. Into this miserable state of affairs stepped the Corsican General Napoléon Bonaparte who, with Paris behind him, staged a coup in 1799.

RIGHT: Built between 1769 and 1772 by architect Jacques Ange Gabriel, the École Militaire was built on the order of Louis XV (prompted by his mistress the famous Marquise de Pompadour). A military academy that trained promising commoners the school's most famous student was Napoléon Bonaparte.

BELOW AND OVERLEAF: Place de la Concorde, originally known as place Louis VX, was begun in 1754 by architect Jacques Ange Gabriel. The largest and grandest of Paris's squares, the central statue of the king was pulled down in 1792 and, now known as the place de Révolution, the square boasted a busy guillotine in its place. Both Louis XVI and Marie Antoinette were executed here. Today, the Classical architecture that surrounds the square remains though the guillotine is long gone, replaced by fountains and an obelisk from Luxor presented to the city by the viceroy of Egypt in the nineteenth century.

LEFT: Beneath the thirteenth and fourteenth *arrondissements* are a vast network of tunnels that date back to Roman times. During the 1780s a new purpose was found for these excavations; as the new resting place for many of the bodies lying in Parisian cemeteries. Eventually, the remains of over six million people were moved out of Paris's overcrowded and disease harboring cemeteries.

This painting of Paris was executed in 1782 by Théodore Lespinasse. During the reign of Louis XVI the city was Europe's cultural center. The hub of Enlightenment thought, its streets reflected the city's sophistication. Grand boulevards were created and lit by streetlamps, gardens and promenades landscaped. The year after this painting was finished the city would be swept up in the ballooning craze that was bought to the city by the Montgolfiers.

LEFT AND ABOVE: The Champs de Mars, between the Eiffel Tower and École Militaire, was originally a market garden that became a military drilling ground and later a park that has since hosted world's fairs and rock concerts. It was also the site of the battle between the Romans and Gauls that brought Paris under Roman rule in 52BC.

LEFT AND RIGHT: Commissioned by Louis XV as an offering to Ste-Geneviève after he recovered from an illness, the Classically-designed Panthéon became the resting place of Paris's greatest thinkers after the Revolution. Within its crypts are the remains of Victor Hugo, Voltaire, Rousseau, and Zola, as well as Pierre and Marie Curie.

ABOVE: La Villette Rotunda, designed by Claude Nicolas Lédoux, was one of about sixty toll barriers in the Fermiers Généraux tax wall that was built to enclose the city between 1784 and 1791. Hated by Parisians, the wall ensured that tolls and taxes on all goods entering the city were paid.

RIGHT: One of the pivotal points in Paris's evolution as a city was the French Revolution, which started with the storming of the Bastille on July 14, 1789. The king and royal family were imprisoned and eventually executed, beginning a period of almost a century during which the country appointed emperors and kings only to stage another revolution. The political situation in Paris would only become stable with the establishment of the Third Republic in 1871. In terms of the city's growth, Paris all but stagnated until Napoléon Bonaparte came to power in 1799. The fortress itself was quickly torn down and there is little left in the place de Bastille, save a few foundations, to remind Parisians of the prison.

LEFT: The Musée National d'Histoire Naturelle building is surrounded by the Jardin des Plantes that was created in 1635 by Louis XIII. Founded in 1793, during the Revolution, the museum is now one of the world's great museums with branches in many other cities and towns throughout France.

Two Emperors and the Belle Époque: 1800–1913

The first of Paris's iron bridges, Pont des Arts was constructed in 1803 (and rebuilt in 1984). A pedestrian footbridge, it connected the Louvre's Cour Carré and the Institut de France.

Two Emperors and the Belle Époque: 1800–1913

Under Napoleon, who was crowned emperor at Notre Dame in 1805, Parisian architecture took on a Classical look as befitted a rival to Ancient Rome. From his court at the Tuileries, the emperor oversaw new grand projects, including the Bourse, the Madeleine, the Arc de Triomphe du Carrousel (at the entrance to the Palace of the Tuileries), and—of course—his tribute to his own martial prowess, the Arc de Triomphe. In addition, Napoleon—ever the crowd-pleaser—began to make some improvements to the city's infrastructure, including the Canal de l'Ourcq and the Canal St-Martin, which increased water supply to the city. The overcrowded and unsanitary old cemeteries were emptied of their occupants and new cemeteries, including Père Lachaise created further from the city center, while the bones of about six million people were placed in the city's Roman catacombs. Streets such as Rue de Rivoli, Boulevard Malesherbes, and Avenue de l'Observatoire were widened and the square before Notre Dame enlarged for his coronation. More streets acquired gaslights and the houses along them were given numbers for the first time.

With Napoleon's defeat at Waterloo in 1815 came decades as unrest as the country swung between monarchy and revolution. Though some notable structures (Pont Louis Philippe and Pont du Carrousel for example) date to this period it was generally one of unrest—punctuated by a cholera epidemic that killed 20,000—during which few could foresee the glorious times that were ahead.

When Napoléon's nephew Louis-Napoléon was elected to power in 1848, he used his position as president of the French Republic to stage a *coup d'etat* and, like his uncle before him, declared himself emperor of France. Prompted by his fear that Paris would rise in revolution again, under Napoleon III the city was completely transformed. As the Industrial Revolution gathered pace, the city's population boomed once more and to cope with new technologies such as the railroad, Baron Georges-Eugène Haussmann was commissioned to rebuild Paris as a modern, magnificent city.

To accomplish his task, Hassmann demolished about sixty percent of the existing city, slashed through old districts with wide new boulevards to facilitate traffic, created modern sewage and water plants, raised schools and hospitals, created parks, and opened railway stations.

In a rapid turn of fortunes, when the emperor was captured and deposed by the Prussian army during an ill-planned war, Paris swiftly descended into the chaos of the 1871 Commune, during which thousands lost their lives and fire razed many of the city's buildings.

RIGHT: The Academy of the Fine Arts building of Institut de France in St-Germain-des-Prés occupies the site of the medieval Nesle Tower. The institute has been the home of the five academies that form the institute since 1805.

Nevertheless, with its last revolution over, the city quickly regained its feet and the decades up until World War I were ones of peace and prosperity during which Paris again led the world in science and the arts. Although the city had blazed a trail with exhibitions of new technology in 1798, it was the series of exhibitions held in the city during the latter half of the nineteenth century that are chiefly remembered today. Fairs held in 1839, 1844, and 1849 had become increasingly larger and by the time that the 1855 exhibition opened thirty-four countries were represented within the specially constructed Palais d'Industrie on the Champs Elysées. Crowning all were the final fairs of the century in 1878, 1889, and 1900. The world's attention was focussed on Paris and the city was left with a host of new constructions—such as the Eiffel Tower, Pont Alexander III, and the Métro—that remain integral parts of the city today.

RIGHT: Today the world's most visited cemetery, Père Lachaise was designed in 1804 by the architect Brogniart. Among its famous graves are those of Paris's famous lovers Abélard and Héloïse, whose remains were joined in a specially designed tomb in 1817, as well as Molière, Oscar Wilde, Sarah Bernhardt, Colette, Edith Piaf, and rock singer Jim Morrison.

Standing on the Place du Carrousel is the Arc de Triomphe du Carrousel. Built between 1806 and 1808, it was designed by Charles Percier and Pierre Léonard Fontaine and commemorates France's many victories of 1805.

The Pont du Carrousel is one of the city's best known and well loved bridges. Built between 1831 and 1834 and designed by Antoine-Rémy Polonceau, it joins the Quai des Tuileries to the Quai Voltaire.

Established by Napoleon in 1804, the Père-Lachaise cemetery covers nearly 119 acres and is the largest cemetery in the city. It houses the tombs of Oscar Wilde and Jim Morrison among others.

RIGHT: Created by merging three farms in 1824, Montparnasse Cemetery is one of the most famous in the world and is the final resting place for many of France's famous authors and artistes.

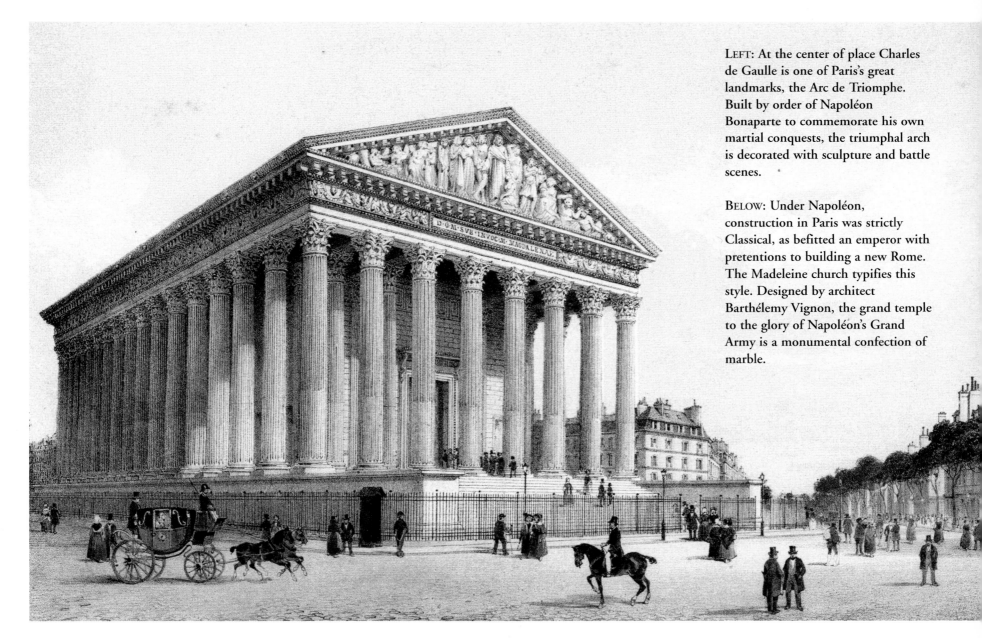

LEFT: At the center of place Charles de Gaulle is one of Paris's great landmarks, the Arc de Triomphe. Built by order of Napoléon Bonaparte to commemorate his own martial conquests, the triumphal arch is decorated with sculpture and battle scenes.

BELOW: Under Napoléon, construction in Paris was strictly Classical, as befitted an emperor with pretentions to building a new Rome. The Madeleine church typifies this style. Designed by architect Barthélemy Vignon, the grand temple to the glory of Napoléon's Grand Army is a monumental confection of marble.

LEFT: Built on the order of Napoléon to help supply parts of Paris with water, Canal St-Martin opened in 1825. Lined with trees and crossed by footbridges, the canal is now a popular destination.

RIGHT: Another of Napoléon's Classical additions to Paris is La Bourse, the city's stock exchange, which was designed by Alexandre Brogniart and opened in 1826. This photograph dates to around the turn of the century.

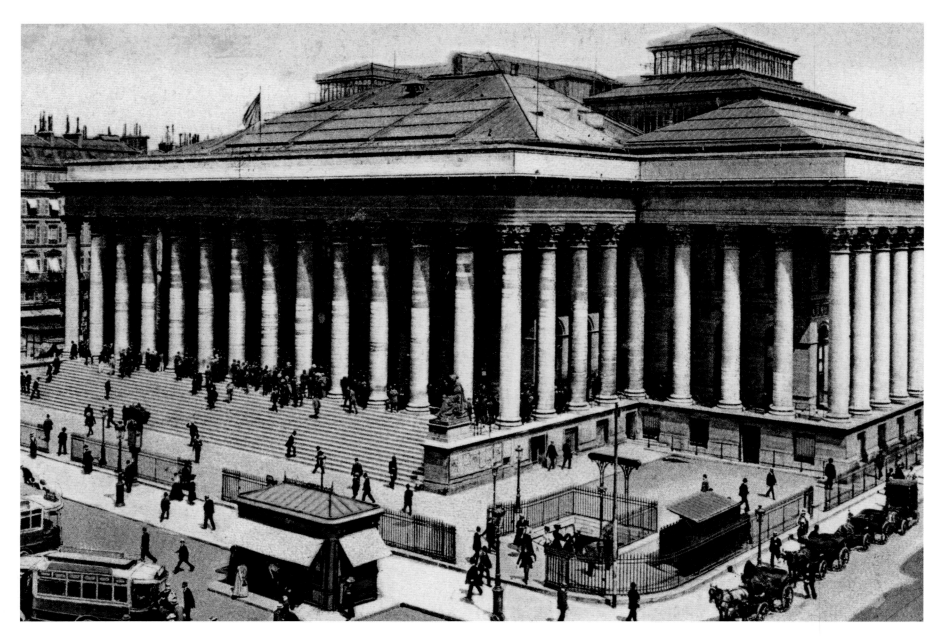

LEFT: The Paris Stock Exchange, historically known as "La Bourse" is pictured in this postcard from 1919. The stock exchange has had many homes including the Palais Brongniart.

ABOVE: The impressive dome of the Bourse de Commerce, otherwise known as Palais Brongiart, designed by architect Alexandre-Théodore Brongniart.

BELOW AND RIGHT: The Elysées Palace, just off the Champs Elysées on the Rue du Faubourg Sainte-Honoré, has been the official home to the President of the Republic since 1848.

LEFT AND RIGHT: In 1853 Napoleon III appointed Baron Georges-Eugène Haussmann *Préfet de la Seine* and charged him with the improvement of the city, which was struggling to cope with a population that now numbered in excess of a million and whose network of medieval streets were laborious to traverse for a city that was now at the center of a growing rail network. Haussmann's response was to plan what he considered the most modern and beautiful city in the world. These two contemporary etchings show the extent to which Paris was torn down to make way for the new streets and buildings.

LEFT AND RIGHT: Along the way Haussmann destroyed about sixty percent of the original city, but left a Paris of broad boulevards, ornate Second Empire architecture, and grand vistas as well as new schools, hospitals, and residential districts. Parks were landscaped and water and sewage systems constructed. In effect, modern Paris was created within a few decades under the guidance of just one man and a handful of architects. The black and white illustrations shows the place de l'Étoile (now the place Charles de Gaulle) remodeled to give views of the Arc de Triomphe, and the new Les Halles marketplace

LEFT: The Pont de Bercy was originally a suspension bridge built to replace a struggling ferry service. The wooden suspension bridge was replaced in 1863 by a more sturdy stone structure.

RIGHT: Just one of the many administrative buildings for each of Paris' arrondissements. Until 1860, Paris had just 12 separate arrondissements but Napoleon III reorganised the territory and since then there have been 20.

ABOVE: The existing Gare du Nord rail terminal was designed by the architect Jacques Ignace Hittorff and built between 1861 and 1865 to replace the city's first small rail terminal that had been raised in 1846 and quickly rendered obsolete by the volume of rail traffic. The façade is dominated by an ornate arch and twenty-three statues that symbolize the cities that were reached by the Chemin du Fer du Nord rail company. To keep pace with demand for rail travel, further additions and improvements were made in 1884 and 1889 and during the 1930s and 1960s.

One of the largest and oldest railway stations in Paris, the Gare de l'Est was opened in 1849. It was renovated many times over the following decades and, by 1931, it had doubled in size, changing the surrounding neighborhood considerably.

The main entrance of the Gare du Nord. Today the station is busier than ever, since the introduction of the Eurostar it is possible to travel all over Europe from here.

ABOVE: A bird's eye view of the 1867 exhibition grounds, which occupied nearly seventy hectares of the Champs de Mars and Île de Billancourt. Forty-one countries were represented at the fair with 52,000 individual exhibitors. At the center was the enormous exhibition palace, which was designed to resemble the Roman Colosseum.

LEFT AND RIGHT: Palais Garnier represents the height of Second Empire opulence. Designed as a stage for opera by Charles Garnier in 1862, the building is highly ornate inside and out, featuring a wealth of statuary (including Carpaux's famous *La Danse),* gilt, mirrors, chandeliers, marble, and rich fabrics. Recently restored, it still stages opera and ballet productions to this day. The black and white photograph dates to the end of the nineteenth century, a decade or two after the opera house opened.

BELOW AND RIGHT: Even today, the Palais Garnier remains one of the most impressive and decadent buildings in Paris, hosting many internationally important musical events.

LEFT: Commanding sensational views over the city from the top of the butte Montmatre, Sacré Coeur is one of Paris's most visible and beloved landmarks. Built by public subscription as an act of penance following the Franco-Prussian War, the first stones were laid in 1871 and the church was completed in 1914.

RIGHT: The Fountain Coutan and Central Dome of the 1889 exhibition, which celebrated a century since the Revolution. Perhaps the most famous of Parisian World's Fairs, the exhibition was presided over by the newly built Eiffel Tower.

LEFT: A view of the majestic interior of the Basilica of Sacré Coeur in Montmartre.

RIGHT: All that remains of the once beautiful Tuileries Palace are the peaceful formal gardens designed by Andre Le Notre back in 1664. The palace itself was destroyed in 1871 during the suppression of the Paris Commune although recently efforts are being made to support reconstruction.

172

LEFT AND RIGHT: The last of Paris's nineteenth century revolutions occurred in 1871 when the Commune of Paris was declared at the Hôtel de Ville on March 26. By April, Paris was a city of barricades and street fighting between the Communards and the Versaillais forces of the French Assembly. During the battles and following the victory of the Assembly forces, buildings and entire streets were set ablaze by the Communards, including the Hôtel de Ville (later restored) rue de Rivoli, Tuileries Palace, and many other government buildings. The contemporary illustration shows the streets of Paris on fire during hostilities, while the black and white photograph is of the Hôtel de Ville after it was torched by fleeing Communards.

LEFT: The aftermath of the "semaine sanglante" or Bloody Week on the Champs Elysses. Parisians led the uprising in protest of the Franco-Prussian War and in the wake of the fighting Napoleon III's government and many buildings lay in tatters.

RIGHT: The ornate "Église de la Sainte-Trinité" was built in 1867 as part of Baron Haussmann's plan to beautify Paris. Designed by Theodore Ballu, La Trinité cost almost 4 million francs to complete.

177

26 MARS 88 N 31

ABOVE, RIGHT AND FAR RIGHT: Two photographs showing the Eiffel Tower under construction and a contemporary, hand-colored, photograph taken soon after building was completed. The first (ABOVE) shows the superstructure at the first level, the four legs united by massive horizontal girders. In the second image (RIGHT) the partially built Eiffel Tower awaits its crowning tower shaft. The tower was designed by Gustave Eiffel and, at over 1,000 feet high, was the tallest structure in the world when it was opened by King Edward VII of England in time for the 1889 exhibition. Now a universally recognized landmark and a symbol of Paris, the tower was not always so well-liked. At the time of construction, many Parisians, including names such as Maupassant, Emile Zola, and eminent architect Charles Garnier, objected to its construction.

179

LEFT: In the center of the Place de la République stands a great monument dedicated to the newly formed republic and designed by the Morice brothers, Léopold and Charles. The final version of the bronze sculpture was inaugurated in 1883.

RIGHT: Designed by Jean Resal the "Pont Mirabeau" was built in iron between 1893 and 1896. Each side of the bridge is decorated by symbolic statues. This statue represents the "Ville de Paris" descending into the Seine.

LEFT AND RIGHT: The infamous Moulin Rouge cabaret opened its doors in 1889 in the Pigalle red light district on the Boulevard de Clichy near Montmartre. A notorious den of iniquity famous for the red windmill on its roof, sparkling electric lights, and the depravity that could be found within, the "Red Windmill" is a popular tourist attraction to this day.

7304 The "Moulin Rouge" the "warmest" place in Paris.

FOLLOWING PAGE: Today's superb art museum, the Musée d'Orsay, was originally a train station built to cope with the influx of visitors for the 1900 exhibition. Designed by Victor Laloux it narrowly escaped demolition in the 1950s and was renovated during the 1970s.

LEFT: The impressive exterior of the Musée Orsay as seen from the banks of the Seine.

ABOVE: Sitting on the banks of the Seine is the Tribunal Correctionel. It is here where many internationally important trials are held.

LEFT: Pavilions representing various countries at the Paris Exposition of 1900 line the Rue des Nations along the Seine River. Attracting over fifty million people, the exhibition was one of the most successful in history and looked back over a century of progress and achievement.

RIGHT: The first line on the Paris Métro system, the *Maillot-Vincennes,* was opened during the 1900 World's Fair. The famous Art Nouveau entrances were the work of architect Hector Guimard.

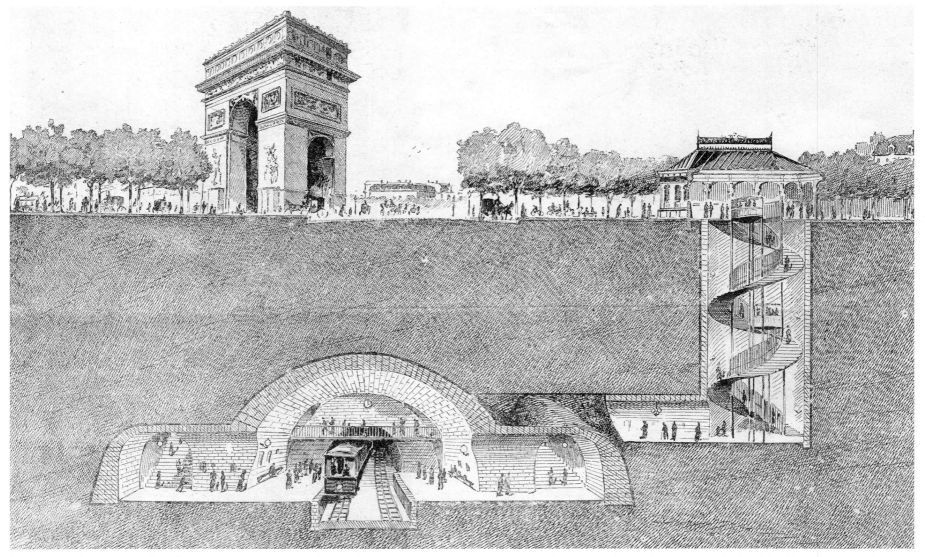

LEFT: An early diagram of the burgeoning metropolitan line underneath Paris. Dating from 1895 this simple illustration shows the Étoile Metro Station underneath Place Charles de Gaulle.

RIGHT: An aerial shot of the Paris exposition in 1900 looking across to the Eiffel Tower and surrounding pavilions of the Rue des Nations.

LEFT: Visitors hurry toward the Trocadero Palace during the exhibition of 1900.

RIGHT: The main entrance of the Grand Palais. It is a little known fact that the Grand Palais has its own police station situated in the basement to protect some of the more valuable exhibits.

BELOW AND RIGHT: The Grand Palais and Pont Alexandre III both date to the 1900 exhibition. The bridge connects the exhibition buildings to the Hôtel des Invalides on the Left Bank and is richly ornamented with sculptures and lampposts.

FAR LEFT: A detailed photograph showing the architectural adornments of the Grand Palais.

LEFT: This exquisite Art Nouveau interior was designed by Alphonse Marie Mucha in 1900 for the Parisian jeweler, Georges Fouquet. The interior has been reconstructed in the Musée des Arts Decoratifs to preserve its beauty and artistic importance.

LEFT: A panoramic view of the Trocadero Palace as it stands today.

BELOW AND RIGHT: The facade and interior gardens of the Petit Palais. Built for the Exhibition of 1900, this building now houses the "Musée des Beaux-Arts de la Ville de Paris".

ABOVE AND RIGHT: Paris contains some of the most exquisite examples of Art Nouveau architecture to be found anywhere in the world. These two examples show the doorways to Castel Beranger (ABOVE), designed in 1901 by Hector Guimard, who was also resonsible for Paris's famous Art Nouveau Métro stations, and the apartment building at 29 avenue Rapp by Jules Lavirotte (RIGHT).

LEFT: Built by the Paris-Lyon-Mediterranean Company in 1900 for the World Exhibition, Le Train Bleu Restaurant in the Gare de Lyon has become a world famous place for tourists and gastronomes alike.

Aerial view of Paris, c. 1909.

The Place de la Concorde, c. 1909.

LEFT: The view of modern day Paris, looking out over the Trocadero Palace and fountains from the first level of the Eiffel Tower.

LEFT: The famous clock tower of the Gare de Lyon is considered to be similar in style to the clock tower of Big Ben in London. The entire station was built for the Exhibition of 1900.

RIGHT: The city has recovered well from the destruction of 1871 as this photograph of Montmarte Boulevard in 1900 will attest.

LEFT: One of the first working Metro stations in 1900 is pictured here. The immediately recognisable Art Nouveau sign by Guimard would soon become world famous.

RIGHT: The Viaduct d'Austerlitz was built in 1904 solely as a railroad bridge. It links the Gare d'Austerlitz on the left bank to the Quai de la Rapée on the opposite side of the Seine.

Modern Paris: 1914–Today

Modern Paris: 1914–Today

The Belle Époque was brought to a swift end by the advent of World War I, and the following depression and the city's occupation by the German Army during World War II brought expansion and growth to an effective halt for thirty years. In fact, by the end of World War II, the city's population was roughly the same as at the beginning of the century.

When hostilities ceased in 1945, Paris quickly recovered as it had done so many times before, though the following years were not without problems. As the population began to increase dramatically, new low-income housing projects began to sprawl around the outskirts of the city, and areas were razed in the rush to provide solutions for the housing shortage. Nevertheless, Paris's historic districts escaped the brutality of quick-build fifties and sixties apartment buildings.

Outside the city center, Paris modernized, notably with the creation of La Défense, which would become a treasure trove of modern architecture and the largest planned buisness district in Europe. As the memories of occupation receded and Paris stabilized, the city regained some of its old *joie de vivre*. Under President Georges Pompidou, the city welcomed the architecturally outstanding Centre Pompidou and his successor, Valery Giscard d'Estaing, initiated a new park—La Villette—and transformed the old Gare d'Orsay into a superb art museum. When François Mitterand came to power he launched new projects, such as the Louvre Pyramid and the Grand Arche de la Défense.

With the city center now strictly protected to the point where some fear that the city center might become one large museum, Paris's architectural and cultural heritage looks to be quite safe. At the beginning of the new millennium it is the city suburbs that are most likely to carry the torch of Parisian growth and development into the future.

RIGHT: Paris's first skyscraper was constructed in 1973. At 689 feet the Tour Montparnasse was the tallest building in Europe at the time and remains the tallest in France.

LEFT AND RIGHT: The Grande Mosquée de Paris was completed in 1926 and originally founded as a sign of gratitude to the Muslim fighters from the colonies who fought against the Germans during World War I.

FAR LEFT: The world famous café, "Les Deux Magots" in Saint-Germain-des-Pres helped cement Paris' reputation as a center of café culture and the arts. It was here that great thinkers, writers and artists of the twentieth century would meet, including Picasso, Sartre, and Hemmingway.

LEFT: The Pont de Bir-Hakeim was completed in 1905 and is the second bridge to occupy this site. Originally named the "Pont de Passy", it was renamed in 1948 to commemorate the Battle of Bir-Hakeim where Free French forces clashed with the Nazi Afrika Korps.

LEFT: The last historic movie theater in Paris with an original auditorium, Le Grand Rex was built in 1937 and is the largest of its kind in the city.

RIGHT: Paris offers many of the world's best examples of Art Nouveau architecture. This apartment building in the center of the city has been lovingly restored and preserved.

LEFT AND PAGES 228–229: In 1958, the French government decided to renovate the western area of Paris with the building of new offices and apartments, including the suburbs of Puteaux, Courbevoie, and Nanterre. The result is the amazing glass and steel architecture of La Défense at the western end of Paris's "Historical Axis." Containing the city's tallest skyscrapers as well as the monumental Grande Arche, which recalls the Arc de Triomphe, the area constitutes Europe's largest planned business district.

LEFT: This aerial view of the modern day Place Charles de Gaulle shows how well Haussmann's original designs have stood the test of time.

RIGHT: Situated inside the enormous Art Deco building of the Palais de Tokyo is a contemporary art museum. The original building was completed in 1937 and the eponymous museum was opened in 2002.

OVERLEAF: The dramatic view from the top of the Arc de Triomphe looking down the Champs Élysées. Avenues and wide boulevards branch out towards to all major landmarks.

LEFT AND RIGHT: By the 1960s, Paris was struggling in the face of a population explosion that saw hundreds of thousands living in shanty towns on the city's borders. In 1901, official census figures put the population at 2,714,068 living within Paris. By 1962 that figure was 7,384,363. A million of these were Algerians, who flocked to the city when Algeria gained independence in 1960. The government response was to encourage industry to relocate and the building of vast suburbs and housing projects, increasing the size of Greater Paris massively almost overnight.

LEFT: To the northeast of the city near the town of Roissy, is Paris, and France's, air hub. Charles de Gaulle Airport opened in 1974 and is now one of Europe's biggest, handling in excess of fifty million passengers annually.

RIGHT: The postmodern Centre Pompidou was built to a competition winning design by Renzo Piano and Richard Rogers. With much of the fabric of the building (lifts, air-conditioning, etc) on the outside, the interior is a superb space which has areas for performance, exhibitions, and a restaurant.

LEFT AND RIGHT: Les Halles Market Place dates back to 1183 when King Philippe II Auguste enlarged the marketplace and added shelters for the merchants. Huge glass and iron structures were added in the 1850s but by the 1970s the entire market was shut down and dismantled. In its place is the Forum des Halles, an underground modern shopping precinct built during the 1970s.

LEFT AND RIGHT: Work began on La Villette, the second largest green space in Paris, during the 1980s and was designed by innovative planner Bernard Tschumi. Once a slaughterhouse area, it now boasts parks, museums and cinemas.

LEFT: Paris is a city that always embraces new and innovative design, including this ultramodern construction called La Géode, an omnimax theater situated in the Cité des Sciences et de l'Industrie.

RIGHT: Designed by the internationally renowned I.M. Pei, the Louvre Pyramid was commissioned by President François Mitterand and constructed in 1989. The eye-catching entrance to the Louvre galleries, which was immortalized in *The DaVinci Code*, is seventy feet high and constitutes the most recent of additions to the Louvre that have taken place since the time it was simply a bastion in Paris's wall.

OVERLEAF: The bustling and vibrant Latin Quarter in Paris has become one of the cities most popular tourist stops with the winding narrow streets packed full of bistro's, bars, and restaurants.

ABOVE: Opened exactly 200 years after the storming of the Bastille, the Opéra de la Bastille, in the place de la Bastille, is the result of a competition to design the city a new opera house that was won by Carlos Ott. Intended to replace the Opera Garnier, today audiences still like to watch performances in the splendor of the older opera house.

RIGHT: The Bibliothèque Nationale de France François Mitterand was designed by Dominique Perrault and opened in 1996. Much criticized for its 1960s influenced architecture, the corner buildings house books while readers sit underground. The trees on the central sunken courtyard were all transplanted from the grounds of Château Fountainbleu.

LEFT: Designed to be a modern day take on the Arc de Triomphe, La Grande Arche in La Defense was the brainchild of Danish architect Otto von Spreckelsen but was not completed until 1989, two years after his death.

FAR LEFT: The new Ministry of Finance building is situated in Bercy district and was built during the 1980s. Due to the imposing look of the building, it is often referred to as the "Bercy Fortress".

LEFT: The modern and sprawling cityscape of Paris today.

RIGHT: Just one of the many futuristic buildings found at La Defense. This particular tower contains the headquarters for the glass company Saint-Gobain.

LEFT AND RIGHT: The futuristic appearance of the business district of Paris is a far cry from the historic charm of the capital.

RIGHT: The changing face of Paris as it follows the winding path of the Seine. Old buildings slowly give way to the modern until reaching the skyscrapers of the futuristic business district of La Defense.

The view across the business district looking down the wide boulevard that leads directly towards the Arc de Triomphe.

LEFT: Stade de France is situated to the north of Paris in the city of St.-Denis. The stadium, which can seat 80,000 people, opened its doors in January 1998, in time to host the 1998 Soccer World Cup.